NETWORKS

ROUND THE MOUNTAIN

John McInnes, *Senior Author*

John Ryckman

Clayton Graves

NELSON CANADA

© Nelson Canada,
A Division of International Thomson Limited, 1986

Published in 1986 by
Nelson Canada,
A Division of International Thomson Limited
1120 Birchmount Road
Scarborough, Ontario
M1K 5G4

ISBN 0-17-602349-6

Canadian Cataloguing in Publication Data

McInnes, John, 1927-
  Round the Mountain

(Networks)

ISBN 0-17-602349-6

I.   Readers (Elementary).   I. Ryckman, John, 1928-
II. Graves, Clayton.   III. Title.   IV. Series:
Networks (Toronto, Ont.)

PE1119.M257 1985   428.6   C85-098766-0

Printed and bound in Canada

Contents

Hello

by Mary Ann Hoberman

Hello's a handy word to say
At least a hundred times a day.
Without Hello what would I do
Whenever I bumped into you?

Without Hello where would you be
Whenever you bumped into me?
Hello's a handy word to know.
Hello Hello Hello Hello.

You'll Grow into It

If your new jacket is too big,
and the sleeves hide your fingers,
don't worry!
You'll grow into it.

If your new jeans are too big,
and the bottoms drag on the ground,
don't worry!
You'll grow into them.

If your new baseball cap is too big,
and it falls down over your eyes,
don't worry!
You'll grow into it.

If your new book is too long,
and the words are hard to read,
don't worry!
You'll grow into it.

Kindness Is Catching

One morning
Julie was getting ready for school.

"Hurry up," her mother called.
"The bus is coming."

"I can't hurry up," said Julie.
"My zipper is stuck."

Julie's mother fixed the zipper.

"Thanks, Mom," said Julie.

Her mother hugged her and said,
"Don't forget—kindness is catching!"

Julie met Angelo at the bus stop.
Angelo's arms were full.
Julie helped Angelo get on the bus.

"Thanks, Julie," said Angelo.

"You're welcome," said Julie.
"Don't forget—kindness is catching!"

The bus stopped at the school.
All the children got off.
Amy's hat blew away.
Angelo ran after it.

"Here's your hat," said Angelo.

"Thanks," said Amy.

"You're welcome," said Angelo.
"Don't forget—kindness is catching!"

Brian got off another bus.

Amy ran to the school door.
She held it open for him.

Brian said, "Thanks, Amy."

"You're welcome," said Amy.
"Don't forget—kindness is catching!"

Brian said to Angelo,
"I can carry some of your books."

"Thanks," said Angelo.
"Kindness *is* catching!"

A Long, Long Time Ago

A long, long time ago,
when I was very small,
I couldn't fly my kite.

My best friend helped me
fly my kite.

Flying a kite is easy now.

A long, long time ago,
when I was very small,
I couldn't ride my bike.

My best friend helped me ride my bike.

Riding my bike is easy now.

A long, long time ago,
when I was very small,
I couldn't catch a fish.

My best friend helped me
catch a fish.

Catching a fish is easy now.

A long, long time ago,
when I was very small,
I couldn't swim.

My best friend helped me
learn to swim.

Swimming is easy now.

A long, long time ago,
when I was very small,
I couldn't skate.

My best friend helped me
learn to skate.

Skating is easy now.

Everything is easy
when best friends help you learn.

She'll Be Coming Round the Mountain

Traditional

Let's sing a song about a train!

She'll be coming
round the mountain
when she comes.
Toot! Toot!

She'll be coming
round the mountain
when she comes.
Toot! Toot!

She'll be coming
round the mountain,
She'll be coming
round the mountain,
She'll be coming
round the mountain
when she comes.
Toot! Toot!

She'll be driving
six white horses
when she comes.
Click, clack!

She'll be driving
six white horses
when she comes.
Click, clack!

She'll be driving
six white horses,
She'll be driving
six white horses,
She'll be driving
six white horses
when she comes.
Click, clack!

She'll be stopping
at the station
when she comes.
Clang! Clang!

She'll be stopping
at the station
when she comes.
Clang! Clang!

32

She'll be stopping
at the station,
She'll be stopping
at the station,
She'll be stopping
at the station
when she comes.
Clang! Clang!

And we'll all go out
to meet her
when she comes.
Yippee!

Yes, we'll all go out
to meet her
when she comes.
Yippee!

34

Yes, we'll all go out
to meet her,
Yes, we'll all go out
to meet her,
Yes, we'll all go out
to meet her
when she comes.
Yippee!

A Friend for Dragon

One morning the teacher said,
"Girls and boys, look what I found
on my desk!"

"It's a note," said Paul.
"I wonder what it says."

The teacher said, "Who can read the note?"

"I can," said Pam. "It says. . .
Wanted
A little, lonesome dragon
wants a friend."

Gino said, "It's from Dragon!"

The teacher said, "I found another note.
Who can read it?"

"I can!" said Darren. "It says...
Dear Dragon,
I will be your friend."

Cheryl said, "It's from Rosie.
Who is Rosie?"

The teacher showed them a new puppet.
"This is Rosie," he said.

"It's a little raccoon," said Stuart.

The teacher said, "How do you think
Dragon feels now?"

"Happy!" said all the children.

Kathy said, "Dragon won't be lonesome
anymore."

R-O-S-I-E

(Sung to the tune of "B-I-N-G-O")

Lonesome Dragon found a friend
And Rosie was her name-O!
R-O-S-I-E,
R-O-S-I-E,
R-O-S-I-E,
And Rosie was her name-O!

Rosie Writes a Story

6

Once upon a time
there was an astronaut.
Her name was Captain Rosie.
Captain Rosie lived in a tree.

7

Astronauts don't live in trees!

This one does.

Room for Three

One morning Dragon went for a walk.
He came to a pond.
He saw Rosie Raccoon.

"What are you doing?" he asked.

"I'm painting a sign," said Rosie.

"What does the sign say?"
asked Dragon.

"Wait and see," said Rosie.

Dragon read the sign,
"ROSIE'S BOAT RIDE.
ROOM FOR THREE."

"Oh, good," said Dragon.
"Will you take me for a ride?"

"No," said Rosie.
"The sign says ROOM FOR THREE
and you are only one.
You need two more to make three."

Just then Squirrel came along.

"Do you want to go
for a boat ride with me?"
asked Dragon.

"Yes," said Squirrel. "I like boat rides."

Dragon said to Rosie,
"Now will you take us
for a boat ride?"

"No," said Rosie.
"The sign says ROOM FOR THREE,
and you are only two.
You need one more to make three."

Dragon and Squirrel went to look
for Skunk.

Skunk was still asleep.

Dragon said, "Wake up, Skunk.
We are going for a boat ride."

"Do you want to come?"
asked Squirrel.

"Yes," said Skunk. "I like boat rides."

Dragon, Squirrel, and Skunk went
to the pond.

"Where's the boat?" asked Skunk.

"Where's Rosie?" asked Squirrel.

"There she is," said Dragon.
"She has three frogs in her boat."

Skunk read the sign.
"ROOM FOR THREE," he said.
"I see four in the boat.
The sign is wrong."

Soon Rosie came back.
The frogs jumped out of the boat.

Dragon said to Rosie,
"Your sign is wrong."

"You're right," said Rosie.
"My sign is wrong. I'll fix it."

Rosie fixed the sign.

Rosie sang,
"Rosie's Boat Ride,
Room for Three,
Dragon, Squirrel, Skunk,
and me!"

Dragon's Dance

Ready, steady,
Here we go.
Turn around once
And say "hello."

Right foot forward,
Left foot too.
Turn around once
And touch your shoe.

Two steps forward,
Count one, two.
Turn around once
And cry "Ya-hoo!"

Snap your fingers,
One, two, three.
Turn around once
And slap your knee.

Clap your hands,
One, two, three, four.
Turn around once
And call for more!

Bow to Dragon.
He's your friend.
Turn around once
And that's the end!

At the Bake Shop

SPECIALTODAY
pumpkin pies — 4
bagels — 5
bread — 6
cookies — 7
doughnuts — 8

MEG & AL'S BAKERY

Four pumpkin pies
fresh from the oven.

Take away three.

How many are left?

Five brown bagels
sprinkled with seeds.

Take away four.

How many are left?

Six loaves of bread
sitting on a shelf.

Take away five.

How many are left?

Seven chocolate cookies
lined up in a row.

Take away six.

How many are left?

Eight jelly doughnuts
ready to eat.

Take away seven.

How many are left?

One pumpkin pie,
one brown bagel,
one loaf of bread,
one chocolate cookie,
one jelly doughnut.

Take them all away.

That's it for today!

Rope and String

HÉLÈNE DESPUTEAUX

79

The Lion and the Mouse

Traditional

One day a lion was sleeping
in the sun.
A mouse came along
and ran over the lion's paws.

The lion woke up
and caught the mouse.

The mouse was frightened.
"Let me go! Let me go!" he cried.
"And someday I will help you."

The lion laughed at the mouse.
"How can a little mouse help
a big lion?"

The mouse said, "You will see."

The very next day,
the lion was walking in the forest.

He got caught in a trap.
"Help! Help!" he cried.

The mouse heard the lion
and ran to help him.

The mouse said, "I will help you.
I will chew the rope
and set you free."
The mouse chewed and chewed
on the rope.
Soon the lion was free.

"You see," said the mouse.
"A little mouse can help
a big lion after all."

"Thank you," said the lion.
"Now I know that a little mouse
and a big lion can be friends."

Old Mother Hubbard

Traditional

Old Mother Hubbard
Went to the cupboard
To fetch her poor dog a bone,
But when she got there,
The cupboard was bare
And so the poor dog had none.

She went to the fish store
To buy him some fish,
But when she came back,
He was licking the dish.

She went to the fruit store
To buy him some fruit,
But when she came back,
He was playing the flute.

She went to the tailor's
To buy him a coat,
But when she came back,
He was riding a goat.

She went to the hatter's
To buy him a hat,
But when she came back,
He was feeding the cat.

She went to the shoe store
To buy him some shoes,
But when she came back,
He was reading the news.

She went to the barber's
To buy him a wig,
But when she came back,
He was dancing a jig.

The Dame made a curtsey;
The dog made a bow.
The Dame said, "Your servant."
The dog said, "Bow-wow!"

Senior Editor: Deborah Gordon Lewi
Editor: Jocelyn Van Huyse
Design and Art Direction: Rob McPhail
Cover Design: Taylor/Levkoe Associates Limited
Cover Illustration: Roger Paré
Typesetting: Trigraph Inc.
Printing: The Bryant Press Limited

Acknowledgements

All selections in this book have been written or adapted by John McInnes, John Ryckman, and Clayton Graves, with the exception of the following:

Hello by Mary Ann Hoberman: Reprinted by permission of Russell and Volkening, Inc. as agents for the author. Copyright © 1974 by Mary Ann Hoberman.

Illustrations

Philippe Béha: 16-26; Brenda Clark: 47-61; Hélène Desputeaux: 76-81; Rowesa Gordon: 4; Margaret Hathaway: 68-75; Vesna Krystanovich: 9-15, 62-67; Roger Paré: 27-35, 82-87; Barbara Reid: 88-95; Tina Seemann: 42-46

Photographs

Ian Crysler: 88-95; Jeremy Jones: 36-41; Helena Wilson: 5-8

9 10 11 12 BP 98 97